DARING TO DREAM AGAIN

OVERCOMING BARRIERS THAT HOLD YOU BACK

...will fly high on wings like eagles. They will run and not grow weary. They will walk and not faint.

Isaiah 40:31

CONTENTS

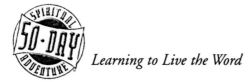

Learning to Live the Word

This Adventure was created with input from pastors and laypersons across North America.

Vision of Mainstay: In this sight and sound culture, our holy task is to help pastors help people grow on Sundays and beyond. To support this vision, Mainstay provides practical tools and resources, including the annual 50-Day Spiritual Adventure, the Seasonal Advent Celebration, and our website: www.teamsundays.org.

Printed in the United States of America
ISBN 1-57849-289-0

03 04 05 06 07 08 09   10 9 8 7 6 5 4

MAINSTAY
MINISTRIES
Leading the Team for
Life-Changing Sundays

Visit our website: **www.teamsundays.org/adventure**

What did you want to be when you grew up?

Many of us had dreams of being astronauts or movie stars or doctors or baseball players. What happened to those dreams? Well, we grew up. Most of us had to adjust to the realities of life. We came up against barriers—we were afraid of heights or couldn't hit a curve ball—and those obstacles kept us from fulfilling our childhood dreams.

Some of us continued dreaming, even though our dreams changed. But others were scarred by the disappointment of those lost goals, or we grew comfortable and complacent, and we stopped dreaming.

God also has dreams, or plans, for us, but many Christians have stopped dreaming with him. Maybe once they imagined their lives could be pure and powerful, energized by God's Spirit. But they smacked into barriers—their own pain or doubt or laziness or blindness. When we stop dreaming, something dies inside us. And when we stop dreaming God's dreams for us, we find our emotions, decisions, and relationships sapped of spiritual vitality.

In this Adventure we invite you to dream again. It takes some courage. Dreams open you up to disappointment, perhaps even ridicule, but they can also bring great joy and satisfaction.

What do you want to be as you grow up in Christ? And what are the barriers that might hold you back? On each of the eight Sundays of this Adventure, we'll focus on a potential obstacle and ways we might overcome it. We'll learn that to dare to dream again, you need to:

1. Let God heal your painful past.
2. Discover God's present involvement in your life.
3. Establish godly goals for your future.
4. Empower everything you do for God with prayer.
5. Confront your ungodly prejudices.
6. Identify with God's heart for the world.
7. Move with God beyond your comfort zones.
8. Believe that with God all things are possible.

You'll also have the opportunity to work on some simple disciplines to help you become the dreamer and believer God wants you to be.

- Are there hurts in your past that keep you from going forward? Healing can begin as you embrace a new, God-given identity.
- Does God seem distant from you? Have fun with the daily God Hunt, looking for specific instances of God's fingerprints in your life.

3

- Do you lack direction in your spiritual journey? A simple acronym can help you set godly goals.
- Are you overwhelmed with all you have to do? Use the short Daring to Dream Again Prayer to ask God for focus and empowerment.
- Have you put walls between yourself and people of other races, classes, or even ages? One of God's marvelous dreams is unity among his people, and he wants us to take steps toward making that vision a reality.
- Are your dreams limited to what God is doing in your own nation? This Adventure can set you on the road to becoming a "world-class Christian."
- Have you been stuck in some comfort zone, afraid to venture out? Daily encounters with God's Word can give you the courage to "go for the gulp."
- When thinking about the future, do you tend to focus on negative outcomes or positive possibilities? By the end of this Adventure, we hope you'll expect great things as you begin to dream again.

Starting to feel intimidated? Don't be. You're not alone in this venture. For more than 20 years, your Adventure planners have been leading similar spiritual forays. Trust their expertise. Don't second-guess their instructions. If they suggest you memorize a short Scripture passage, for example, assume it can be done with minimal effort, yielding maximum value.

This is not a pretend Adventure; it's for real. The fact that hundreds of thousands of fellow believers are on this journey along with you should be an added encouragement.

Going on the Adventure as a church is a great experience when everyone—of all ages—is learning the same things at the same time. (For a simple model to help you get the most out of church, see p. 50.) Maybe your Sunday school class or small group will participate. The mutual accountability and encouragement will be a decided plus.

The Lord is pleased that you have committed yourself to a plan of accelerated, measurable, and lasting spiritual growth. Hopefully, you'll be both surprised and delighted by what the Holy Spirit does in and through you as you cooperate with him. The next 50 days may not fashion you into everything you always wanted to be, but this Adventure can help you get past some barriers and discover the joy of dreaming again, learning to trust God for great things.

Transform Your Life

This is more than an ordinary Bible study you're holding. It's a road map to spiritual growth—a Spiritual Adventure that can literally transform your life. We trust that two months from now, you will have broken through the barriers that inhibit you from dreaming big spiritually.

After finishing the Adventure, you should have established at least one new healthy spiritual habit. If you can accomplish that in a strategic area of your spiritual life, you will have made enormous progress. And that's what this Adventure is all about: accelerating your spiritual growth while developing your relationship with the Lord. So make it your goal to establish at least one new healthy spiritual habit. On page 9 you'll find suggestions for setting a specific Adventure goal.

What tools do I need in order to do the 50-Day Spiritual Adventure successfully?

1. Your Bible. Regular Scripture reading is an important part of this Adventure. Make sure you're using a Bible you understand.

2. This journal. Here is where you'll process what you read in Scripture each day. We offer a few questions to help you get at the meaning of the text and how it relates to your daring to dream again. Key insight: This journal is not an intensive Bible study guide; it's primarily a tool to help you apply scriptural truth to your everyday life. And that's a challenge for everyone!

3. The Adventure Guidebook—*Never Too Late to Dream*, by David R. Mains. This inspiring little book will give you added insights into the eight themes of the Adventure so that you can realize your enormous God-given potential. Read a chapter a week to keep current (reading time: maybe 20 minutes per week). To obtain this resource, go to your church book table, call Mainstay at 1-800-224-2735, or visit our website: www.teamsundays.org/adventure.

What do I need to do?

First, read the suggested Scripture passage each day and answer the questions in this journal. Second, read a chapter every week in the Adventure Guidebook, *Never Too Late to Dream*. And then there are the important application steps. . . .

Why are these application steps so powerful?

The Adventure application steps are practical, proven ways to help you live the Bible's teachings in your daily life. The Word of God is powerful to transform you, when you apply it. The applications will challenge even the seasoned believer and Bible scholar. They are described on the pages following each Sunday (or Saturday/Sunday) in this journal. The eight application steps are called:

1. Take on a healthy new identity.
2. Go on a daily God Hunt.
3. Set godly goals.
4. Personalize the Daring to Dream Again Prayer.
5. Widen your circle of unlikely friends.
6. Become a world-class Christian.
7. Go for the gulp.
8. Begin dreaming again.

How much time is involved?

It generally takes just 10–15 minutes per day to complete the daily journal activities. Reading the guidebook will require an extra 20 minutes per week. You'll also need additional time blocks to complete some application steps. In this aspect of the Adventure, you'll reap what you sow. So don't skimp on the application steps.

How do I keep track of everything?

We'll prompt you throughout this journal to help you keep current with the application steps. Take the Adventure one day at a time, and you'll be fine. For an overview of all the application step assignments, see page 8.

Do I need to follow the journal every day?

You'll get more out of the Adventure if you do. But if you miss a day or two, don't panic! It's best to pick up with the current day, rather than trying to make up what you've missed.

How are the pages organized each week?

Every Sunday (or Saturday/Sunday), a commentary by Dr. David Mains introduces the theme for the coming week and sets the tone for the days ahead. The next pages provide room to take notes on your pastor's sermon, followed by a description of the week's application step. Monday through Friday you'll find further Scripture readings and questions on the theme of the week.

Can I Adventure with my friends or family?

Absolutely. That's a great way to make the study even more meaningful. It will take some extra time as you discuss the Scriptures or review one another's progress, but the mutual accountability and encouragement will be of great benefit. And we provide lots of help with journals for adults, students, and children, along with small group materials. For specific ideas, call Mainstay at 1-800-224-2735, or visit our website (see below).

How can I connect with fellow adventurers in other parts of the country?

Visit our website: www.teamsundays.org/adventure. You'll discover any number of ways to dialogue with Adventure team members nationwide and benefit from what God is doing in their lives.

What can I do to keep going when the Adventure is over?

Once you've finished the Adventure, you undoubtedly will want to continue with the spiritual habits you've developed over these 50 days. One proven method is simply to repeat this Adventure, using a new copy of this journal. That's a great way to solidify your spiritual gains. On pages 76–77 we offer some other suggestions to help you keep growing spiritually.

Where should I start?

Use pages 8–9 to review the spiritual growth opportunities in this journal and to set your personal Adventure goal. You might also flip through the day-to-day section of the journal, beginning on page 10. Then prepare yourself for Adventure Day 1 and a marvelous experience of accelerated, measurable, and lasting spiritual growth.

The following is a summary of the various application steps in the Adventure and when they are to be done. For a full description of the applications, refer to the pages following the Sunday (or Saturday/Sunday) pages in the journal each week. This journal provides weekly and daily reminders to guide you through the various steps.

Daily

- ❑ Study the assigned Scripture passage, and answer the questions in the journal.
- ❑ Track God's present involvement in your life by recording your "God Hunt sightings" on pages 40–41. Begin on Adventure Day 8. (See p. 19.)
- ❑ Empower everything you do for God with prayer by using the Daring to Dream Again Prayer. Begin on Adventure Day 22. (See p. 36.)

Weekly

- ❑ Read the appropriate chapter in the Adventure Guidebook, *Never Too Late to Dream.*
- ❑ Work on memorizing Philippians 3:12–14, the Adventure memory passage.

Once during the Adventure

- ❑ Let God heal your painful past, by taking on a healthy new identity. (See p. 12.)
- ❑ Establish a godly goal for your future, using the suggestions on pages 27–28.
- ☑ Confront your ungodly prejudices by taking steps to widen your circle of unlikely friends. (See p. 45.)
- ❑ Identify with God's heart for the world as you become more familiar with a region, country, or people-group. (See p. 56.)
- ❑ Move with God beyond your comfort zones by completing the exercise starting on page 65.
- ❑ Answer the questions on page 75 to help you begin dreaming again.

The Lord can use the next 50 days to help you establish at least one new healthy spiritual habit, if you let him teach you how. By applying the process of goal-setting to one strategic area of your spiritual life, you can make enormous progress toward becoming more like Jesus during this Adventure. Here are four simple steps to help you do that:

1. Prayerfully ask God which aspect of your spiritual life he wants you to make a priority during this Adventure. For starters, pray through the list of Adventure application steps on page 8.
2. Take ownership of God's response by writing it down as a goal in the space provided (below).
3. Give priority to the appropriate plan of action that will help you reach your spiritual goal.
4. Believe in the power of the Holy Spirit to get you there, and resolve to stick with your plan.

What is the area of your spiritual life in which you believe God most desires to see you mature during the next 50 days? Is it prayer, Bible study, serving others, becoming missions-minded? What specifically would the Lord like to see happen in this area of your life? State that as your spiritual goal.

My goal during this 50-Day Spiritual Adventure is to:

_____

Now consider how this Adventure can help you reach your goal. Review the application step descriptions found on the pages that follow each Sunday in this journal. One or more application steps should provide you with an appropriate plan of action. If you don't find what you need in the journal, create your own plan of attack.

My plan is to:

Be more considerate not to ...

Ask the Holy Spirit to empower you to stick with your plan. Don't get caught in the perfectionist trap. Trust God to work a miracle in your life. Studies show it takes 21 days to establish a habit, good or bad. So this 50-Day Adventure allows you time to get a good habit started and make it stick. Finally, celebrate the progress you make with God's help during the Adventure.

DAY 1 SUNDAY

Theme 1: To dare to dream again, let God heal your painful past

Theme 1 runs Sunday–Friday, Days 1–6

Introduction to Theme 1

Strip people of their dreams and you assign them to lives hardly worth living. Witness what the Taliban did to the people of Afghanistan. In Gideon's day, the Midianites had systematically crushed Israel in a similar fashion.

Gideon had no idea that in God's eyes he was a mighty hero. Even when an angel of the Lord addressed him as such, Gideon had a hard time processing the message. Past and present pain had stolen his hope of an exciting future.

There are too many believers whose present drab spiritual condition is similar to Gideon's mind-set before his remarkable transformation. Memories of hurts of one kind or another have caused these Christians to stop dreaming God's dreams for them.

The Lord wants those individuals to assume new identities, just as Gideon did. God desires that his people envision amazing new possibilities of service because of the miraculous healing touch of his Son. Quite possibly, one of those hidden heroes is you!

Apply the Scriptures

1. What painful past experiences was Gideon nursing?

   _____

2. What arguments did Gideon raise against God's adventure for him?

   _____

3. Describe a time when you felt God was calling you to something you weren't confident you were prepared for.

   _____

4. God gave Gideon the strength to go on his adventure and the promise "I will be with you." How has God encouraged you in the past?

   _____

❑ I have read through the introductory material in this journal (pp. 3–9). The Adventure goal I will work toward is _____

   _____

heme 1: To dare to dream again, let God heal your painful past

Philippians

Not that I have already obtained all this or have already been made perfect, but I press on to take hold of that for which Christ Jesus took hold of me. Brothers, I ask you

Adventure Application 1
Take on a Healthy New Identity

Gideon certainly never pictured himself as a mighty hero. He had heard accounts of God's working in earlier generations, but negative experiences had become a barrier to Gideon's ever dreaming such dreams for his day. Taking on a healthy new identity required some healing and some getting used to, but in the end, he performed his role admirably.

What negative experiences have brought you pain or shame and prompted you to shelve the spiritual desires you once had? Whether the problem was of your own making or the fault of others, it's time to let God heal those wounds. The following steps give you a good start.

1. Put a name to the way you have been living. Is it Fearful Gideon, Resentful Mary, Wounded Curtis, Angry Sally, Disillusioned _____ Negative _____, or _____ _____? Don't move on to step until you have identified the false name under which you have been living.

2. Now ask the Holy Spirit to show you the new name he wants you to embrace. "Mighty hero, the Lord is with you!" is the healthy new identity the angel asked Gideon to accept. What new identity might God want you to receive? *Joyous & humble*

Which of your two titles—the false name (step 1) or the new identity (step 2) do you like best? Which do you want to mark you in the future as you dare to dream again? *hopefully 2*

- Read the daily Scripture passages and answer the questions in this journal.
- Sometime this week, read the introduction and first chapter in the Adventure Guidebook, *Never Too Late to Dream.*
- Begin to work on the Adventure memory passage, Philippians 3:12–14.

MONDAY DAY 2

Theme 1: To dare to dream again, let God heal your painful past

Apply the Scriptures

1. What did Jesus mean when he said the prodigal came to his senses?

   _____

2. What barriers kept the prodigal from thinking he could reclaim his original identity as a beloved son?

   _____

   _____

3. The father in this story represents our heavenly Father. How might you be holding on to a painful past that keeps you from dreaming your heavenly Father's dreams for you?

   _____

   _____

4. Picture yourself in the place of the prodigal, with your heavenly Father running to you with welcoming arms. Describe your feelings.

   _____

   _____

5. What would you say if God asked you, "Are you able to enjoy the fine robe, the fattened calf, the music and dancing—the best I have to offer?"

   _____

   _____

❑ I am reading the introduction and chapter 1 in the Adventure Guidebook, *Never Too Late to Dream.*

Theme 1: To dare to dream again, let God heal your painful past

Apply the Scriptures

1. Sometimes people have painful memories of experiences in religious settings. Feelings of anger or shame often accompany those memories. What emotions do you think Paul felt as he looked back on his pre-Christian activities?

   Shame, regret

2. Describe any negative religious experiences (school, church, cult, etc.) that have stirred similar emotions in you.

   _____

3. Paul's testimony makes it obvious that he had moved beyond his painful past to participate in God's plans for him. What healing might God have in mind for you?

   _____

4. Saul was also called Paul, which means "small or little." Some think he chose this name out of humility, no longer wanting to use the proud name *Saul.* What words describe the healthy new identity you want to take on?

   _____

5. Do you know someone who is having trouble moving past a negative religious experience? How could you help that person?

   That person being me

❑ I have chosen the new name I believe God wants me to embrace for this Adventure (Application 1, p. 12).

   Not yet

WEDNESDAY DAY 4

Theme 1: To dare to dream again, let God heal your painful past

Apply the Scriptures   *Shattered Dreams*

1. When you think about the spiritual wrestling that goes on in your life, what nickname would you give yourself?

   Tipsy Turvey

2. If God renamed you as he did Jacob, what name might he have in mind?

   Seeking Child of God

3. Tradition says Jacob was a strong man before his hip was knocked out of joint. What pain might be required for you to take on your new spiritual identity?

   Supplication + finding answers →

4. If you said, like Jacob, "I will not let you go until you bless me," what blessing from God would you request?

   My family to find fulfillment in the Lord

5. What kingdom dream might God want you to identify with during this 50-Day Spiritual Adventure?

   _____

   _____

☑ I am working on the Adventure memory passage, Philippians 3:12–14.

DAY 5 THURSDAY

Theme 1: To dare to dream again, let God heal your painful past

Apply the Scriptures

1. What negative past experience had become a major barrier in David's spiritual life?

   _____

2. In this psalm, David refers to dreams or desires that are blocked by his sin and the memory of it. What are some of those desires, as expressed in verses 7–15?

   _____

   _____

   _____

3. Are any of David's desires unrealized in your life as well? If so, which ones, and why?

   _____

   _____

4. What options did David have, aside from confessing his sin?

   _____

   _____

5. On a separate sheet of paper, write a prayer of your own. You may wish to express to God your dreams, confess any sin that might be holding you back, ask for strength to follow his vision for you, and so on.

   ❏ I have read the introduction and chapter 1 in the Adventure Guidebook, *Never Too Late to Dream*.

Go Deeper: Read Ephesians 2:1–10 on daring to dream again.

FRIDAY DAY 6

Theme 1: To dare to dream again, let God heal your painful past

Apply the Scriptures

1. According to this passage, what will the Lord give in place of:
   ashes? _____
   mourning? _____
   despair? _____

2. The prospect of a fresh start sounds good to people with a painful past. In these verses, identify at least three kinds of people with a painful past for whom the Lord offers a new beginning.

   _____

   _____

   _____

3. In what ways has God given you new beginnings in times past?

   _____

   _____

   _____

4. How would you describe the state of your spiritual life before you started this Adventure?

   _____

   _____

5. Today's reading is the scripture Jesus used to inaugurate his ministry (see Luke 4:16–21). In what area of your life would you like Christ to give you a fresh start and a healthy new identity?

   _____

❑ I have chosen the new name I believe God wants me to embrace for this Adventure (Application 1, p. 12)

Theme 2: **To dare to dream again, discover God's present involvement in your life**
Theme 2 runs Sunday–Friday, Days 7–13

Introduction to Theme 2

David had been anointed by the prophet Samuel—no small event in his life. On that occasion, the Spirit of the Lord came mightily upon this young man. Even so, there would be years spent as a fugitive fleeing from King Saul before David finally assumed the role of Israel's king.

When God's promises don't quickly unfold, some believers falsely assume he's no longer interested in their lives. David's perspective was just the opposite. He knew a war was being fought in the heavenlies, and he trained himself to look for daily evidences of God's care and protection. These were recorded in his prayers, or psalms. One example is Psalm 57, in which David was probably writing about the cave experience recounted in today's passage.

Are you on the lookout for ways the Lord regularly involves himself in your life? Do you write down your "God Hunt sightings"? Have you learned to sustain your belief in bigger dreams because you see Jesus' goodness to you on a daily basis?

Apply the Scriptures

1. What travel stops (restaurants, gas stations, etc.) have the cleanest restrooms?

   Best (maybe) Donalds

2. Saul chose a travel stop at random, the very cave in which David and his men were hiding. Do you think this was a coincidence? Why or why not?

   No – God meant for
   David to realize he was near

3. David viewed this obvious God Hunt sighting differently than his men did. What were the contrasting opinions?

   _____

   _____

4. Saul should have seen this incident as a God Hunt sighting showing unexpected evidence of God's care. What effect should that have had on his life?

   _____

Theme 2: To dare to dream again, discover God's present
involvement in your life

_____

_____

_____

_____

_____

_____

_____

_____

_____

_____

_____

_____

_____

_____

_____

_____

_____

Adventure Application 2
Go on a Daily God Hunt

David was a young man when the prophet Samuel anointed him for future
leadership. As the years passed, someone less spiritually mature might have
assumed God wasn't interested in him any longer, because David spent most of his
time running for his life. Even so, he wrote about numerous ways God made his

presence known, which kept the dream alive.

Does God ever seem far-removed from you? Most of us would admit there are days and weeks when we just don't feel his presence. At other times, it's amazing to see how God provides and protects. But if we're not looking, we can miss these "sightings" or think of them as mere coincidence. Here are four categories of God Hunt sightings to look for:

1. **An obvious answer to prayer.** God doesn't always give us exactly what we want or expect, but he does respond to our requests.
2. **Unexpected evidence of God's care.** We still get sick and have accidents, but God often works miracles of protection, such as the time you miss that traffic pileup because you forget your wallet and have to go back for it.
3. **Unusual linkage or timing.** You might discover that God stirred a person to pray for you at precisely the moment you were in trouble. These mini-miracles are more common than you might think.
4. **Help to do God's work in the world.** You're puzzling over how to teach your Sunday school class when a friend calls with a tale of woe. You comfort your friend with insights from your research for the lesson, and you use your friend's story as the "hook" for your class discussion.

Open your eyes and see the many ways God shows himself in our everyday experience. We often fail to dream because we don't realize how active God is. But if we see his hand protecting and directing and adjusting and tweaking our lives, it's easier to dream along with him.

From now until the end of this Adventure, watch for a God Hunt sighting every day. These are times when the Lord works in or touches our daily world and *we choose to recognize it to be him.* Again, look for indications of God's involvement in your life in any of these ways: (1) an obvious answer to prayer, (2) unexpected evidence of his care, (3) unusual linkage or timing, or (4) help to do his work in the world.

Record your sightings on the chart on pages 40–41. From time to time, reread your entries to remind yourself of how active God has been as he encourages you to dare to dream again.

- Keep current with your daily journal pages, and read chapter 2 in *Never Too Late to Dream,* the Adventure Guidebook.
- Continue to embrace the new name you believe God has given you (Application 1, p. 12).
- Work on the Adventure memory passage, Philippians 3:12–14.

As Abram and Sarai begin their new adventure, God renames them. Now Abram will be known forevermore as Abraham ("ancestor of a multitude"), and Sarai is given the name Sarah ("woman of high rank"). It is an important moment in their lives, even though it comes at such an advanced age. God is inviting them to become someone totally new and to live into a vision of a nation yet unborn.

No doubt, the nine months of Sarah's pregnancy must have given them both time to begin to imagine themselves as the ones God saw them to be. Clearly, they lived up to their new names, and all of Hebrew and Christian history grows out of that miracle.

How powerful it is to embrace a name! God claims us by naming us: "I have called you by name, you are mine" (Isa. 43:1). We claim the best in children when we shape them by naming their good qualities and behaviors. We claim parts of ourselves that we want and own by naming them. There is real power in saying, "I am competent and caring," instead of using negative words like, "I am simply no good at this, and I can't do it!"

Might a Lenten discipline emerge for you from this line of thinking? What is your most positive aspiration for yourself? If you could select a name for yourself, what would it be? Can you imagine being called that name by God? What would it be like to "adopt" that name for the remainder of Lent?

Take some prayer time to bring yourself quietly into God's presence. Imagine that God comes to you, and invites you into a surprising new chapter in your life. By what name do you hear God calling you? What does it feel like to be loved that deeply?

ꓯONDAY DAY 9

ꓱeme 2: To dare to dream again, discover God's present involvement in your life

ꓱply the Scriptures

1. What chain of events led to Paul's rescue from a threat on his life?

_____

_____

2. What might cause you to think that what happened was more than coincidental?

_____

_____

3. It's impossible to prove this was more than a coincidence. Why is it important to *choose* to recognize God's involvement in circumstances like these?

_____

_____

4. Describe a time when you have been in a situation that could have been a coincidence but more likely was God's involvement in your life.

_____

_____

5. What value could you gain by recording God Hunt sightings for the rest of the Adventure (see p. 19)?

_____

_____

❏ I am recording my God Hunt sightings on pages 40–41.
❏ I am reading chapter 2 in *Never Too Late to Dream.*

Theme 2: **To dare to dream again, discover God's present involvement in your life**

Apply the Scriptures

1. Do you think that seeking God is intended to be a one-time experience or daily occurrence? Use a verse from this passage to support your answer.

   _____

   _____

2. Review the four kinds of God Hunt sightings on page 20. Summarize them below.

   _____

   _____

   _____

   _____

3. Put a star by the kinds of sightings that relate to this passage.

4. In verses 9–11, Jesus likens a parent's care for a child to our heavenly Fathe care for us. How could the God Hunt help you develop a childlike trust in the Lord?

   _____

   _____

5. Sometime today, tell someone about a God Hunt sighting you've had, or as that person to share a sighting with you. When you have spoken with some one, check the box below.

❑ I have spoken with someone about a God Hunt sighting.

Go Deeper: Read Lamentations 3:22–26 on daring to dream again.

WEDNESDAY DAY 11

heme 2: **To dare to dream again, discover God's present
        involvement in your life**

pply the Scriptures

1. When have you prayed for success in a task you felt God had asked you
   to do?

   _____

2. Were you surprised by the outcome? Why or why not?

   _____

   _____

3. Describe the kind of stress Abraham's servant must have felt as he faced his
   assignment.

   _____

   _____

4. How might this account be an example of all four categories of God Hunt
   sightings?

   An obvious answer to prayer: _____

   Unexpected evidence of God's care: _____

   Unusual linkage or timing: _____

   Help to do God's work in the world: _____

5. Review verses 26–27. What kinds of God Hunt sightings might Abraham
   have seen in these events?

   _____

   _____

❑ I have read chapter 2 in *Never Too Late to Dream.*

Theme 2: **To dare to dream again, discover God's present
involvement in your life**

Apply the Scriptures

1. On a scale of 1–10 (10 being highest), how would you rate your sense of
   God's involvement in your life as a compassionate Father (verse 13)?

   _____

2. Are there verses in this psalm that refer to personal dreams you hope God w
   yet fulfill? What are those dreams?

   _____

   _____

3. The psalmist, David, encourages us not to forget God's benefits. Which ben
   fit in this psalm stirs a memory of a God Hunt sighting in your life? (See p.
   19 to review the God Hunt.)

   _____

4. How is keeping track of your God Hunt sightings in this journal similar to
   what David is doing in this psalm?

   _____

   _____

5. David begins and ends this psalm by saying, "Praise the Lord, O my soul"
   (NIV). Now that you've been tracking your God Hunt sightings for a few da
   what words of praise would you offer to the Lord?

   _____

   _____

❑ I am getting used to the new name God has given me (Application 1, p. 12

FRIDAY DAY 13

Theme 2: To dare to dream again, discover God's present
involvement in your life

Apply the Scriptures

1. Recall a time when you went into a situation especially aware that you were dependent on God's help.

   _____

   _____

2. In this account, Ezra finally sees a lifelong dream fulfilled: to return with a group of exiled Jews to their native land. They travel with all their wealth through hostile territory. What do they do to prepare for the risks of the journey?

   _____

3. In verse 31, Ezra records the date his people begin this journey during which they will see God's great provision. How do you suppose their children and grandchildren benefited from Ezra's biblical record of their God Hunt sightings?

   _____

   _____

4. How might your family and others benefit from your God Hunt record in the months and years to come?

   _____

   _____

5. Name a stressful situation you're currently facing for which special prayer and/or fasting would be in order.

   _____

❑ So far I have memorized _____ verses from Philippians 3:12–14.

Theme 3: To dare to dream again, establish godly goals for your future
Theme 3 runs Sunday–Friday, Days 14–20

Introduction to Theme 3

Judas was no dummy. He could recognize a great opening when it came his way. Jesus was undoubtedly the long-awaited Jewish Messiah, and Judas was given the unique privilege of being one of the Twelve chosen to be closest to this worker of miracles. Talk about a chance to dream some really big dreams. Here was the opportunity of a lifetime.

Unfortunately, it wasn't long before Judas began to realize that he and Jesus differed about the role the *Christ* (a Greek word), or the *Messiah* (the same word in Hebrew), was to play. Because Judas was unable to give up his self-centered desires, an irreparable breach occurred in their relationship. Satan took advantage of the situation, and the rest is history.

When you set goals for your life, it's extremely important to begin by going to God for input. And, of course, his desires always need to come before your own.

Apply the Scriptures

1. For three years, Judas had been an integral part of Christ's unfolding kingdom dream. Yet, what became a bigger priority to him?

   _____

2. When God's dreams for us become our dreams as well, how should that affec our attitude toward money?

   _____

   _____

3. What did Judas miss by giving in to his self-centered desires?

   _____

   _____

4. Greed literally dominated the life of Judas. What is something in your life that could potentially crowd out Christ's kingdom dream?

   _____

5. What godly goal could you set to overcome this barrier (see p. 27)?

   _____

   _____

Theme 3: To dare to dream again, establish godly goals for your future

_____

_____

_____

_____

_____

_____

_____

_____

_____

_____

_____

Adventure Application 3
Set Godly Goals

As the months of following Jesus passed, Judas came to realize that his dreams and Christ's dreams were different. Money and power were not bottom-line concerns in the kingdom of God. Unfortunately, this member of Jesus' original Twelve set aside godly goals and let the barrier of self-centered desires prompt him to make a tragic mistake.

Goals, whether stated or unstated, need to be regularly checked to see if they are consistent with Christ's desires. This acronym helps simplify that process.

- **G**et God's input
- **O**wn it
- **A**pply it
- **L**ive it
- **S**eek God's input again

Get God's input. "Don't act thoughtlessly," cautions Paul in Ephesians 5:17, "but try to *understand* what the Lord wants you to do" (italics ours). Are your dreams consistent with God's wonderful plans for your life? The writer of Hebrews quotes Christ as saying, "I have come to do your will, O God" (10:7). Ask God to reveal his desires for your life.

Own it. Fix in your mind God's answer. Here are some examples: *God wants me to be a holy person. Jesus wants me to read the Bible every day. The Lord wants me to help someone in need this week.* Psalm 37:23–24 reads, "The steps of the godly are directed by the Lord. He delights in every detail of their lives. Though they stumble, they will not fall, for the Lord holds them by the hand." Tell God repeatedly that his goals are important to you. Make them your own by accepting and believing them. Write them down and put them in a place where you will see them often. You may want to begin with just one goal.

Apply it. Lay out some initial plans for meeting your God-given goals, and begin putting them into action. Start living what you eventually want to become. According to James 1:23, if you hear from God and don't respond in kind, "it is like looking at your face in a mirror but doing nothing to improve your appearance." And in John 13:17 Jesus says, "You know these things—now do them! That is the path of blessing." Ask God to empower you to do what he wants you to do.

Live it. Keep working on realizing your godly goals until they become a way of life. In time, your dream and who you are should be inseparable. "For God is working in you, giving you the desire to obey him and the power to do what pleases him" (Philippians 2:13). When the time is right, share your goals with a friend.

Seek God's input again. There is so much to experience in Christ that you will never be able to learn everything. But the upward call of God is worth a lifetime of pursuit. In Philippians 3:12 Paul writes, "I don't mean to say that I have already . . . reached perfection! But I keep working toward that day when I will finally be all that Christ Jesus saved me for and wants me to be."

Now is the time to learn how to set godly goals. Begin by getting God's input. Start thinking and praying about this matter until you can say with conviction, "I believe I have God's input. My godly goal for the present is:

_____."

- Keep current with your daily journal pages, and read chapter 3 in the Adventure Guidebook, *Never Too Late to Dream.*
- Continue to embrace the new name you believe God has given you (Application 1, p. 12).
- Record your daily God Hunt sightings on the chart on pages 40–41 (Application 2, p. 19).
- Continue memorizing Philippians 3:12–14, the Adventure memory passage.

MONDAY DAY 16

Theme 3: To dare to dream again, establish godly goals for your future

Apply the Scriptures

1. From verses 6–8, trace the unselfish steps of Christ.

_____

_____

_____

_____

2. Christ's ultimate dream (verses 10–11) was to bring glory to God the Father. Realizing what he had to go through to make that happen, describe your feelings toward him in a prayer that begins, *Lord, I thank you for unselfishly . . .*

_____

_____

_____

3. Paul writes that our attitude should be the same as that of Christ Jesus (verse 5). How are your attitudes like or unlike Christ's?

_____

_____

_____

4. What godly goal could you set that would bring glory to your heavenly Father (see p. 27)?

_____

_____

❏ I am recording my God Hunt sightings on pages 40–41.
❏ I am reading chapter 3 in *Never Too Late to Dream.*

Theme 3: To dare to dream again, establish godly goals for your future

Apply the Scriptures

1. Jesus was telling his disciples about the traumatic events that awaited him in Jerusalem. What were they?

_____

_____

2. In that context, what inappropriate request reveals that James and John were giving priority to self-centered dreams?

_____

_____

3. Identify a past or present experience when you have struggled with self-centered desires.

_____

_____

4. According to Jesus, who is great in the unfolding dream of his kingdom?

_____

5. What are some possible ways you could be a servant in the next 24 hours?

_____

_____

❏ I believe I have God's input on a godly goal (Application 3, p. 27).

WEDNESDAY DAY 18

Theme 3: To dare to dream again, establish godly goals for your future

Apply the Scriptures

1. How does this passage show that Christ was affirming his Father's plan as his own?

_____

_____

2. Choose some phrases from this passage that show the tension Christ experienced in submitting to his Father's will.

_____

_____

3. Christ wanted his disciples to share his burden. When have you felt alone as you pursued God's desires for you?

_____

_____

4. Do you know anyone struggling with a God-given goal who needs your support? How might you encourage that person?

_____

_____

5. What is a godly goal you have established? What support do you need to carry it out?

_____

_____

❏ I still have _____ verses to memorize in Philippians 3:12–14.
❏ I have read chapter 3 in *Never Too Late to Dream.*

Theme 3: **To dare to dream again, establish godly goals for your future**

Apply the Scriptures

1. List several lessons you can learn from this passage about godly goals.

    a. _____

    b. _____

    c. _____

    d. _____

    e. _____

2. What specific godly goal do you feel the Lord wants you to set?

    _____

    _____

3. What is a reasonable time-frame for completing it?

    _____

4. Who is someone in the body of Christ with whom you could share your goal and ask for prayer support?

    _____

❏ I believe I have owned my godly goal by writing it down and putting it in a place where I will see it often (Application 3, p. 27).

Go Deeper: Read Psalm 37:1–7a on daring to dream again.

FRIDAY DAY 20

Theme 3: To dare to dream again, establish godly goals for your future

Apply the Scriptures

1. Name some people you admire for setting and achieving high goals.

_____

_____

_____

2. What is Paul's goal, as stated in this passage?

_____

_____

3. According to surveys, most Christians do not have goals for their spiritual lives. Why do you think that is?

_____

_____

4. Review this week's application on page 27. Where are you in the process of setting a godly goal?

_____

_____

5. What prize (verse 14) will make attaining your goal worth all the effort?

_____

_____

❑ I am feeling more comfortable with the new name God has given me (Application 1, p. 12).

Theme 4: To dare to dream again, empower everything
you do for God with prayer
Theme 4 runs Sunday–Friday, Days 21–27

Introduction to Theme 4

Even when you know you have a lot to be thankful for, life has a way of stealing your joy. Certain feelings of inadequacy can sometimes reduce you, like Hannah, to tears. If you're not careful, this ongoing attrition will also rob you of your spiritual dreams.

Our heavenly Father is keenly aware of his children's limited resources. That's why he graciously offers his personal help. God encourages men and women to share with him their deepest spiritual longings. And he doesn't turn away even from a barren woman's desperate prayers for a son.

It's foolhardy to try to fulfill God's desires for you simply through your own efforts. A flurry of activity is never a substitute for serving in tandem with the living Lord. That's why sessions spent conferring with him are not a waste of time. Have you discovered the joy of being empowered by God in all you do for him?

Apply the Scriptures

1. What is a dream over which you've anguished in prayer as Hannah did?

   _____

2. In what ways were your actions like Hannah's, and in what ways did they differ?

   _____

   _____

3. What selfless offering did Hannah make to God? How did she keep her word?

   _____

   _____

4. What might God be waiting to hear from you?

   _____

5. What prevents you from daring to dream that God will answer your prayers as he did Hannah's?

   _____

SERMON NOTES

Theme 4: **To dare to dream again, empower everything you do for God with prayer**

_____

_____

_____

_____

_____

_____

_____

_____

_____

_____

_____

_____

_____

_____

_____

_____

_____

_____

_____

_____

_____

_____

_____

Adventure Application 4
Personalize the Daring to Dream Again Prayer

Hannah's barrenness had made her life miserable. In her desperation, she came to see God as her only hope. At Shiloh she dared to dream again, making a bold offer to the Lord: "Grant me a son, and I will give him back to you." The Lord responded with a miracle child she called Samuel, which meant, "heard by God."

With the birth of Hannah's special son, her offering him back to God for a lifetime of service, and then watching him grow in his work for the Lord, she must have felt she not only knew God's will for her life, but that her greatest dreams had come true.

Unfortunately, many Christians do not experience the same sense of satisfaction. The following prayer is intended to help you in the process of personally partnering with God and recognizing his blessing on all you do.

The Daring to Dream Again Prayer

Lord and Master, as your servant I sincerely want to please you. I don't need to know your plans for my entire life, so help me focus on today. To the best of my ability to discern, this is what I sense are your expectations: _____

_____

Please empower me to serve you in this way. I want your dreams for me to be my dreams as well. Amen.

Use this prayer every day until the end of the Adventure. It should set you on a path of learning to empower everything you do for God with prayer.

It's usually easier to see a few days ahead than to see a few years into the future, to say nothing of a few decades. Hopefully the four remaining weeks of the Adventure will give you a sense—as Hannah had—that you have been heard by God. And that experience can prepare you to see bigger dreams fulfilled in the months and years to come.

- Keep current with your daily journal pages, and read chapter 4 in *Never Too Late to Dream*.
- Continue to embrace the new name you believe God has given you (Application 1, p. 12).
- Record your daily God Hunt sightings on the chart on pages 40–41 (Application 2, p. 19).
- Start applying your godly goal: make a plan of action (Application 3, p. 27).
- Finish memorizing Philippians 3:12–14, the Adventure memory passage.

MONDAY DAY 23

Theme 4: To dare to dream again, empower everything you do for God with prayer

Apply the Scriptures

1. How do the demands and expectations on Christ's earthly life compare to yours?

   _____

2. In the midst of the world's overwhelming needs, how did Jesus stay focused on the dream he shared with his Father?

   _____

3. What lessons can you learn that will help you spend quality time in prayer?

   _____

   _____

   _____

4. What help did Christ receive that day from spending time with his Father?

   _____

   _____

5. What benefits might you expect this week from using the prayer on page 36?

   _____

   _____

❑ I am praying daily the Daring to Dream Again Prayer (p. 36).
❑ I am reading chapter 4 in *Never Too Late to Dream*.
❑ I am starting to put my godly goal into action (Application 3, p. 27).

Go Deeper: Read Proverbs 3:5–6 on daring to dream again.

Date:

Theme 4: **To dare to dream again, empower everything you do for God with prayer**

Apply the Scriptures

1. This passage reminds us that there's a force standing against God's dream and all those aligned with it. How does Paul describe that force?

_____

_____

2. According to the text, what do Christians need to do in order to stand firm in this struggle?

_____

3. As you pray the prayer on page 36, how might the enemy try to thwart what you believe are God's expectations for you in the next 24 hours?

_____

_____

4. What does this passage say each of the six pieces of armor represents?

belt _____

body armor _____

shoes _____

shield _____

helmet _____

sword _____

5. What advantage does prayer add that the other six virtues don't offer?

_____

_____

❑ I am completing my Scripture memory work (Philippians 3:12–14).

WEDNESDAY DAY 25

Theme 4: To dare to dream again, empower everything you do for God with prayer

Apply the Scriptures

1. In the Book of Acts, power is often given to help believers witness about Christ. How is that use of power evident in this passage?

_____

_____

2. For what self-centered purposes do some people in the church today seek empowerment?

_____

_____

3. For what purposes do you generally seek God's empowerment?

_____

_____

4. For what kingdom work do you sense God wants to empower you?

_____

5. In this passage, the believers prefaced their petition with praise. What words of praise would you say to precede the request you listed above?

_____

_____

_____

❑ I am praying daily the Daring to Dream Again Prayer (p. 36).
❑ I have read chapter 4 in *Never Too Late to Dream.*

GOD HUNT SIGHTINGS

For more information on the God Hunt, see page 19.

Sunday, Day 8 _____

Monday, Day 9 _____

Tuesday, Day 10 _____

Wednesday, Day 11 _____

Thursday, Day 12 _____

Friday, Day 13 _____

Saturday, Day 14 _____

Sunday, Day 15 _____

Monday, Day 16 _____

Tuesday, Day 17 _____

Wednesday, Day 18 _____

Thursday, Day 19 _____

Friday, Day 20 _____

Saturday, Day 21 _____

Sunday, Day 22 _____

Monday, Day 23 _____

Tuesday, Day 24 _____

Wednesday, Day 25 _____

Thursday, Day 26 _____

Friday, Day 27 _____

Saturday, Day 28 _____

Sunday, Day 29 _____

Monday, Day 30 _____

Tuesday, Day 31 _____

Wednesday, Day 32 _____

Thursday, Day 33 _____

Friday, Day 34 _____

Saturday, Day 35 _____

Sunday, Day 36 _____

Monday, Day 37 _____

Tuesday, Day 38 _____

Wednesday, Day 39 _____

Thursday, Day 40 _____

Friday, Day 41 _____

Saturday, Day 42 _____

Sunday, Day 43 _____

Monday, Day 44 _____

Tuesday, Day 45 _____

Wednesday, Day 46 _____

Thursday, Day 47 _____

Friday, Day 48 _____

Saturday, Day 49 _____

Sunday, Day 50 _____

DAY 26 THURSDAY

Theme 4: To dare to dream again, empower everything you do for God with prayer

Apply the Scriptures

1. Picture yourself as one of the disciples in verse 31. Use four words to describe your feelings.

   _____

   _____

2. How would you have responded to Christ's invitation, "Come with me by yourselves to a quiet place and get some rest"?

   _____

   _____

3. What barriers in your life sometimes keep you from accepting Christ's invitation to go with him to a quiet place?

   _____

   _____

   _____

4. Choose a place free from distraction where you can be with Jesus.
   The next time I sense Jesus calling me to come away to a quiet place, I will go to _____.

5. What issues would you like to talk with the Lord about in that quiet setting?

   _____

   _____

   _____

❏ I am recording my God Hunt sightings on pages 40–41.
❏ I am beginning to live out my godly goal (Application 3, p. 27).

FRIDAY DAY 27

Theme 4: **To dare to dream again, empower everything
            you do for God with prayer**

Apply the Scriptures

1. After being beaten and shackled, Paul and Silas prayed and sang hymns.
   What would you have done?

   _____

2. God Hunt sightings often come in the context of empowered praying. If Paul
   and Silas had recorded the earthquake as a "sighting," which categories might
   they have put it under (see p. 20)?

   _____

   _____

3. Verses 33–34 report that the jailer washed the men's wounds and set a meal
   before them. What categories of God Hunt sightings fit that situation for
   Paul and Silas?

   _____

   _____

4. If Paul and Silas had taught the jailer to go on a God Hunt, under which categories would he have recorded his conversion experience?

   _____

   _____

5. One never knows what a day might bring. How could the Adventure prayer
   on page 36 prepare your heart for unexpected things God might do?

   _____

   _____

❑ I am feeling more comfortable with the new name God has given me
   (Application 1, p. 12).

Theme 5: To dare to dream again, confront your ungodly prejudices
Theme 5 runs Sunday–Friday, Days 28–34

Introduction to Theme 5

Cornelius was a seeker open to God's truth. Peter had not only spent more than three years in the company of the Man of Truth, he witnessed the resurrected Christ. But the two men would never have met if God had not challenged Peter, a Jew, to confront his prejudices against Gentiles such as Cornelius.

The word *prejudice* implies a judgment that's been made before all the facts are known. And the fact is that God loves all people, not just certain ones. This is a lesson many still need to learn. The people of your particular ethnic background or church group or economic status or race are not the only individuals for whom God has deep feelings.

Peter needed to widen his circle of associations. So might you! Maybe God knows that the dream you are daring to birth requires the help of some unlikely new friends.

Apply the Scriptures

1. List as many God Hunt sightings as you can find in this narrative.

    _____

    _____

    _____

2. What prejudicial barrier was God challenging Peter to overcome?

    _____

3. Peter realized that God's dream included all kinds of people. We all have prejudices, whether we realize it or not. What is one God might want to challenge in your life?

    _____

4. When has this ungodly prejudice shown itself recently?

    _____

    _____

❑ I am reading chapter 5 in *Never Too Late to Dream.*
❑ I have completed my Adventure memory work (Philippians 3:12–14).

SERMON NOTES

_____

_____

_____

_____

_____

_____

_____

_____

_____

_____

_____

_____

_____

_____

_____

_____

_____

Adventure Application 5
Widen Your Circle of Unlikely Friends

Peter had restricted his preaching of the gospel to a limited audience. God helped him overcome the barrier of ungodly prejudice so that the message of forgiveness through Christ could be heard beyond Jewish settings. Peter needed to learn that God's dream for everyone required this servant's widening his circle of unlikely friends. Here's how you can do that, too.

1. **Identify a group of people you have shut out of your life.** Some of us don't picture ourselves as prejudiced, but sometimes we're not sensitive to our blind spots. Might any of these be a problem for you?
   - Racism
   - Sexism
   - Denominationalism
   - Prejudice based on age, marital status, economic or educational level, political persuasion, and so on

   In some churches, members who volunteer to teach Sunday school or sing in the choir, for example, look at those who don't volunteer as being less committed to the Lord. Some Christians write off people who smoke or drink, are overweight or don't seem clean, as being unworthy of their love and attention. You might consider those kinds of prejudice, too.

   Choose one group to focus on during the Adventure. Pray about it. Ask God to soften your heart. And don't play it safe. Try to respond to what the Holy Spirit is telling you.

2. **Examine the reasons behind your prejudice.** Often we can break down our walls by breaking down our thought patterns. There are false "facts," misunderstandings, and illogical conclusions behind our prejudicial attitudes.

   Consider the group you have selected and ask yourself, *When do I feel this prejudice? What reasons do I have to mistrust or avoid people of this race, age, gender, denomination, and so on?* Be honest with yourself. You might have reasons such as:
   - They seem sneaky.
   - They do odd things.
   - I believe their behavior is sinful.
   - I'm afraid of them.
   - They have different values.
   - I've had a bad experience with someone of that group.

   Review the reasons for your prejudice before the Lord. Do they reflect God's viewpoint? He may assure you there's no reason to be afraid of people in a certain group, but he may confirm your conviction that their behavior is sinful. Still, he may urge you to show love to the sinner even while rejecting his or her sinful ways.

3. **Select a person from the group and begin praying for that individual.** Maybe it's a member of your church, or possibly it's a neighbor or someone you pass on the street each day. You might find it easiest to choose another Christian, although that's not necessary. Whoever it may be, begin to pray daily for this person.

4. **At an opportune time, let the person know that he or she has been in your prayers.** What a surprise it can be to have someone say, "I've been praying for you." Now you can ask, "Is there anything specific I can be praying for?"

   Best case: The person shares a request, and you take a step toward friendship. He or she may even offer to pray for you.

   Average case: The person doesn't open up much but accepts your prayers. Don't force the issue. Let God do his work.

   Worst case: You receive a negative reaction. Sometimes "I'm praying for you" sounds like, "You have a problem." Respond as lovingly as possible. If you can clear up a misunderstanding, do so. If not, you may want to choose someone else to pray for.

5. **Consider how your own behavior might need to change.** Is there some aspect of your interaction with this person that demonstrates prejudice? You've taken a big step by praying for someone you've been prejudiced against, but maybe you need to change in other ways as well. Ask the Lord to help you set a specific behavioral goal. "I will/will not do this: _____." Ask God also for the ability to accomplish your goal and to dream new dreams in this aspect of your life.

- Keep current with your daily journal pages, and read chapter 5 in *Never Too Late to Dream.*
- Continue to embrace the new name you believe God has given you (Application 1, p. 12).
- Record your daily God Hunt sightings on the chart on pages 40–41 (Application 2, p. 19).
- Keep working on living out your godly goal (Application 3, p. 27).
- Pray daily the Daring to Dream Again Prayer (Application 4, p. 36).

DAY 30 MONDAY

Theme 5: **To dare to dream again, confront your ungodly prejudices**

Apply the Scriptures

1. Nathanael revealed a prejudice when he asked if anything good could come out of Nazareth. What might be a similar comment people make today?

_____

_____

2. How might Nathanael's initial prejudice have kept him from participating in God's great dream?

_____

_____

3. What did Nathanael gain by letting go of his prejudice?

_____

_____

4. What are ways you sometimes write people off because of where you perceive they are "coming from"?

_____

_____

5. How might you be hindering God's dream for you by writing off those people?

_____

_____

❑ I have identified a group against which I am prejudiced (Application 5, p. 45).

TUESDAY DAY 31

Theme 5: To dare to dream again, confront your ungodly prejudices

Apply the Scriptures

1. List several places where someone might come in contact with people of other ethnic groups.

2. Recall a time when you thought about someone of a different ethnic or age group in a way that embarrasses you now.

3. When have you treated a similar person (see above) in a Christlike way?

4. For you to live in a manner consistent with this passage, what are some ways you can put into practice the proper attitude toward people of other ethnic or age groups?

5. Whom could you express Christlike love to this week to widen your circle of unlikely friends?

❑ I am examining the reasons for my prejudice (p. 46).

Get the Most Out
of Church on Sundays

Spiritual growth most often occurs when we remember God's Word and apply it over time. Since we cannot become what we cannot recall, it's vital that we take steps to remember the sermons and Sunday school lessons we hear at church. They convey the Word of God to us. That's just the first step, though, because it takes more than recollection to be transformed spiritually. What we know is worth little compared to what we do with what we know. So, we must put our faith into practice. James calls it becoming doers of the Word. When we remember God's Word *and* apply it to our lives, we begin to experience the fruits of a transformed life.

These two simple, yet profound, steps can help you turn routine Sundays into life-changing encounters with the risen Lord.

1. **The Preparation Step.** Ask yourself this question weekly:
   What can I do *before, during, or after church on Sunday* to help me remember and apply God's message?

2. **The Follow-up Step.** Attend church looking for the answers to the following four questions:
   • What is God saying to me?
   • What does he want me to do?
   • How do I do it?
   • How long will it take?

These two steps empower you to connect with God in church on Sundays. Use step 1 to fully prepare yourself for what God has to say to you. Use step 2 to discover his specific Sunday message for your life. When you do hear God speak to you, and you understand the answers to the four questions above, write them down so that you won't forget them. Accept and believe what God says to you. Refer to your notes regularly so you'll remember to keep applying them to your life. If you live out this new behavior long enough, it will become an essential part of you. Eventually, you may share your story with someone else. Use both steps to hear God speak to you in church on Sundays. Watch his words transform your life completely as you apply them over time.

When you follow this "Mainstay Model," the words of the Apostle Paul to the Colossians should ring true:

This same Good News that came to you is going out all over the world. It is changing lives everywhere, just as it changed yours that very first day you heard and understood the truth about God's kindness to sinners.—**Colossians 1:6**

WEDNESDAY DAY 32

Theme 5: To dare to dream again, confront your ungodly prejudices

Apply the Scriptures

1. What problem was Paul addressing?

_____

_____

2. The principle of unity in the body could be applied to denominational differences today. When might those differences hinder the fulfillment of Christ's dream for his church?

_____

_____

3. It is important to hold firm to the essentials of the Christian faith. Yet within that framework, denominational prejudices still exist. What are some examples?

_____

4. Name some ways you have grown in your appreciation for the diversity of the body of Christ.

_____

_____

5. How could you gain exposure to a different Christian tradition this week (read an article, go to a website, watch a religious TV program, etc.)?

_____

_____

❏ I am reading chapter 5 in *Never Too Late to Dream*.
❏ I have selected someone to represent the group against which I am prejudiced and have started to pray for that person (p. 46).

Theme 5: **To dare to dream again, confront your ungodly prejudices**

Apply the Scriptures

1. In verse 27, why were the disciples surprised?

   _____

2. If you found your pastor talking with a woman like this in a public place, what would be your response?

   _____

   _____

3. This passage addresses two prejudices of Jesus' day that he did not buy into. What are they?

   _____

   _____

4. The Samaritan woman was used significantly by the Lord. Who is a contemporary woman you can picture God using to further his purposes?

   _____

5. Do you ever have trouble accepting spiritual guidance from someone of the other gender? If so, what are your reasons?

   _____

   _____

❑ I am recording my God Hunt sightings on pages 40–41.
❑ I am praying daily the Daring to Dream Again Prayer (p. 36).

Go Deeper: Read Ephesians 3:14—4:3 on daring to dream again.

Date: _____

FRIDAY DAY 34

Theme 5: **To dare to dream again, confront your ungodly prejudices**

Apply the Scriptures

1. If you had to classify yourself as either the rich or the poor of the earth, in which category would you place yourself?

   _____

2. When do you come in contact with people who are poor?

   _____

3. What does James say a Christian attitude should be toward those who are poor?

   _____

   _____

4. What barriers keep you from following this teaching?

   _____

   _____

   _____

5. Name a poor person who may be in need of your encouragement.

   _____

❑ I am living out my godly goal (Application 3, p. 27).
❑ I am becoming more comfortable with the new name God has given me (Application 1, p. 12).

Theme 6: To dare to dream again, identify with God's heart for the world
Theme 6 runs Sunday–Friday, Days 35–41

Introduction to Theme 6

We're more like Jonah than most of us care to admit. For example, how would you respond if God clearly called you to minister in Mongolia?

Don't laugh. God loves Mongolians just as much as he loves North Americans. He wants the millions who live there to experience his mercy and grace, even though we might have trouble locating Mongolia on a world map. Is it hard to believe that God's plans include a time when revival fires will sweep across that vast part of Asia?

It's impossible to know God well without identifying with his heart for the lost of the world. Don't be like Jonah, who agreed to the Lord's wishes only when presented with much less desirable options.

Jonah never really overcame the obstacle of his provincialism. But you can dream God's dreams for a needy world. Look for places where the spiritual harvest is ripe. Become a world-class citizen!

Apply the Scriptures

1. Have you ever had a major disagreement with God? Explain.

   _____

2. What was the disagreement between God and Jonah about?

   _____

3. God had a dream for Nineveh, the capital of pagan Assyria, Israel's avowed enemy. Why do you suppose this prophet was reluctant to participate in that dream?

   _____

4. In what specific ways do God's people today sometimes think like Jonah?

   _____

5. Name a contemporary country that Christians think of as pagan, where God is doing a marvelous work.

   _____

❏ I am reading chapter 6 in *Never Too Late to Dream*.

SERMON NOTES

Theme 6: To dare to dream again, identify with God's heart for the world

_____

_____

_____

_____

_____

_____

_____

_____

_____

_____

_____

_____

_____

_____

_____

_____

_____

_____

_____

_____

_____

_____

_____

_____

_____

_____

_____

_____

_____

_____

Adventure Application 6
Become a World-class Christian

Jonah didn't like the Assyrians and resisted preaching repentance in their capital city. When God called him to hold this crusade, Jonah bolted. To get his prophet to fulfill his desires for Nineveh, the Lord overcame numerous barriers. Even then, Jonah proved less than world-class, missing the ripe harvest and failing to identify with God's heart for the world.

By Saturday (Adventure Day 42):

1. **Choose the region, country, or "people-group" with which you would like to become more familiar.** For example, you might want to focus on a region such as the Middle East, a specific country like Saudi Arabia, or a particular group such as Palestinians in Israel.

2. **Start praying for your region, country, or people-group.** Believe that God can work in the lives of those you're learning about. Ask him to help you see what he sees in this part of the world.

Then in the weeks that follow:

3. **Gather information. Start a file about your area of focus.** Become more familiar with this part of the world. Find out what God is already doing there. Here are some items you might include in your file.

    • Newspaper or magazine articles, or summaries of news stories you see on television or on the Internet.
    • Information on how people from your focus area celebrate important

holidays. If you need help, your local reference librarian should be able to point you in the right direction.

- Newsletters from missionaries working in your focus area. If you don't already receive them, your pastor or church office staff can give you names of organizations to contact.
- Your reflections on a festival or other special event you attend in an ethnic neighborhood (if you live in a multicultural area).
- Notes on what you learn by helping a child with a school project on a foreign country.
- Your reaction to a movie, video, or TV special you watch about your area of interest.

Try to accumulate at least six items in your file by Day 50 of the Adventure. Make this assignment fun. You might even include recipes of foods you try or your response to music you listen to from the part of the world you've targeted.

4. **Seek avenues for meeting people from your focus area.** Check the Yellow Pages for ethnic churches or clubs you could visit. If you're near a college or university, they may be able to put you in contact with international students. Perhaps you could invite one to your home for a meal. Or, you might befriend an international you see regularly in the bank or grocery store. Allow these cross-cultural contacts to help you learn more about other countries.

5. **Personalize ways in which God might involve you in his dreams for your interest area.** Perhaps you could begin corresponding with a missionary or contributing to his or her work. Maybe you and your family could sponsor a child living in the place you've been studying. God might even give you the opportunity to visit your focus area. Be open to his surprises as you dare to dream again.

- Keep current with your daily journal pages, and read chapter 6 in *Never Too Late to Dream*.
- Continue to embrace the new name you believe God has given you (Application 1, p. 12).
- Record your daily God Hunt sightings on the chart on pages 40–41 (Application 2, p. 19).
- Continue to live out your godly goal (Application 3, p. 27).
- Pray daily the Daring to Dream Again Prayer (Application 4, p. 36).
- Continue to widen your circle of unlikely friends; tell the person you are prejudiced against that you are praying for him or her (Application 5, p. 45).
- Work on becoming a world-class Christian (Application 6, p. 56).

Theme 6: **To dare to dream again, identify with God's heart for the world**

Apply the Scriptures

1. Write down four nations you've heard or read about recently in the news.

   _____

   _____

2. As you reread Psalm 96, include one of those countries whenever you see the word *nations*. Example: "Declare his glory among the nations *[such as Japan]*, his marvelous deeds among all peoples" (NIV).

3. What do you think are some of God's dreams for the countries you listed above?

   _____

   _____

   _____

   _____

4. What is a hymn or chorus that has the same theme as this psalm?

   _____

5. List some possible nations or people-groups you might choose to identify with (see Become a World-class Christian on p. 56).

   _____

   _____

❏ I am praying daily the Daring to Dream Again Prayer (p. 36).
❏ I have chosen a region, country, or people-group with which I will become more familiar (Application 6, p. 56).

Date: _____   Read **Matthew 28:16–20**

TUESDAY DAY 38

Theme 6: To dare to dream again, identify with God's heart for the world

Apply the Scriptures

1. If you had been with the disciples at this time, how well equipped would you
   have felt to carry the gospel to the world?

   _____

2. When you hear the word *missions,* what is your initial response?
   ❑ No interest
   ❑ Little interest
   ❑ Some interest
   ❑ Significant interest
   ❑ Great interest

3. In this passage, Christ gives a promise that would help his disciples. Another
   promise is found in Acts 1:7–8. What are they?

   _____

   _____

4. List several potential barriers you imagine the disciples would have to overcome to help fulfill Christ's dream for the world.

   _____

   _____

5. Had the disciples focused on their own country and nothing beyond, most of
   us probably would not be Christians. What might be the results if today's
   Christians fail to identify with God's heart for the world?

   _____

   _____

❑ I have told the person against whom I am prejudiced that I'm praying for
   him or her (Application 5, p. 45).

Theme 6: **To dare to dream again, identify with God's heart for the world**

Apply the Scriptures

1. Who is someone you know who exemplifies verse 15?

   _____

2. What reminder would help you pray on a consistent basis for that person?

   _____

3. Think about a country, area, or people-group with whom you are considering identifying (see p. 56). If you had been born in that setting, how would your life be different from the way it is now?

   _____

   _____

4. In the setting you pictured for question 3, what would need to take place for God's dreams to be realized in your life?

   _____

   _____

5. It is estimated by the U.S. Center for World Mission that there are 10,000 people-groups that still remain unreached by the gospel. This represents several billion people. What part can you play in helping them hear the gospel?

   _____

   _____

❑ I am recording my God Hunt sightings on pages 40–41.
❑ I am starting to pray for my chosen region, country, or people-group (p. 56).
❑ I have read chapter 6 in *Never Too Late to Dream*.

THURSDAY DAY 40

Theme 6: To dare to dream again, identify with God's heart for the world

Apply the Scriptures

1. Have you ever sensed that God was trying to communicate with you through a dream? If so, what was he attempting to show you?

   _____

   _____

2. In today's passage, Paul and his companions, deeply involved in God's dream of preaching the gospel throughout the world, take a different direction. What God Hunt sighting caused them to change their course?

   _____

3. Explain how this God Hunt sighting could possibly fit all four categories below.

   An obvious answer to prayer: _____

   Unexpected evidence of God's care: _____

   Unusual linkage or timing: _____

   Help to do God's work: _____

4. As you pray about an area, country, or people-group to focus on for Adventure Application 6, what direction do you feel God is giving you?

   _____

❑ I am praying daily the Daring to Dream Again Prayer (p. 36).
❑ I am feeling more comfortable with the new name God has given me (Application 1, p. 12).

Go Deeper: Read Philippians 1:1–6 on daring to dream again.

DAY 41 FRIDAY

Theme 6: **To dare to dream again, identify with God's heart for the world**

Apply the Scriptures

1. In the Gospels, Christ shared with his disciples what seemed an impossible dream: that all the world would hear about him. What does today's passage reveal about the fulfillment of Christ's dream?

   _____

   _____

2. Picture yourself among this multitude, seeing people from every nation praising God. What three words describe your feelings?

   _____

   _____

3. According to this passage, what role did Christ play in bringing these people together?

   _____

   _____

4. What part can you play in reaching all nations, tribes, peoples, and languages?

   _____

   _____

5. How has this Adventure helped you become more of a global Christian? (Examples: awareness, prayer, etc.)

   _____

   _____

❑ I am gathering information about my chosen region, country, or people-group (p. 56).

How to Turn Your New
Spiritual Habits into a Lifestyle

You're about to begin the last week of the 50-Day Spiritual Adventure. Completing this journey is no small accomplishment. You may be spending more time than usual in God's Word. Maybe you're empowering your life through prayer. Perhaps you've taken on a healthy new identity or are widening your circle of unlikely friends. With one week to go, this is a good time to review where you've been and consider where you want to go next.

What has God done in your spiritual life over the last six weeks? If you set a personal goal for the Adventure (p. 9), think about your progress. Are you pleased with what's happened? Or do you need a fresh start?

Now ask the Lord to show you the next step he would have you take in your spiritual life. Even if you've made great progress toward your goal, you may find yourself challenged again once the 50 days are over. You'll need an action plan to help you keep pursuing your objective. And if you haven't identified a spiritual goal, why not seek God's direction as the Adventure draws to a close.

My spiritual goal for the time following the Adventure is to:

_____

One way to continue progressing toward your goal is simply to get a fresh copy of this journal and repeat the Adventure. This allows you to cement the spiritual habits you've formed and make them part of your ongoing lifestyle. If you're ready for a fresh challenge, try one of the other Spiritual Adventures shown on pages 76–77 of this journal. Of course, you may have another plan for working toward your goal. If so, by all means follow it! Whatever you choose as your next step, you should find helpful information and support at our website: www.teamsundays.org/adventure.

My action plan is to:

_____

_____

Finally, as you did when you began this Adventure, ask the Holy Spirit to enable you to stick with your plan. It can take several months to establish a spiritual habit—and another several months to turn it into a lifestyle. But if you resolve to move steadily toward your goal, you'll see the benefits of a life transformed by Christ's daily presence.

Date:

Read **Luke 1:26–38; 2:33–35; John 19:25b–2?**

DAY 42 SATURDAY
DAY 43 SUNDAY

Theme 7: To dare to dream again, move with God beyond your comfort zones
Theme 7 runs Sunday–Thursday, Days 42–47

Introduction to Theme 7

People who are comfortable with their life seldom aspire to anything greater. Often what prompts change is the awareness that our experience should be better.

In early New Testament times, Roman rule left the Jews with much to be desired. Talk of the long-awaited Messiah surfaced frequently. Even so, Jews had to be careful about what they said and to whom they spoke.

Gabriel's announcement to young Mary had all kinds of ramifications. She had responded to God's angel by saying, "I am willing to accept whatever he wants." But the more her life unfolded and the more she saw the profound impact her decision had made, the more Mary must have gulped.

In order for her people to dare to dream again, the mother of Jesus had to repeatedly move outside her comfort zones. And so must most of us if we are to fill the various roles God has in mind for our lives.

Apply the Scriptures

1. Name several ways Gabriel's message to Mary must have moved her beyond her comfort zones.

2. If you said to the Lord what Mary said to Gabriel, what might be God's response?

3. Describe what you might think and feel if someone shared with you this word from the Lord: "A sword will pierce your very soul."

4. This prophecy was fulfilled for Mary, especially at the Crucifixion. In contrast, what were some benefits of her accepting her role as the Lord's servant?

5. What are potential positive aspects of your being willing to accept whatever God wants for your life?

Theme 7: **To dare to dream again, move with God beyond your comfort zones**

_____

_____

_____

_____

_____

_____

_____

_____

_____

_____

_____

Adventure Application 7
Go for the Gulp

Mary must have gulped when the angel announced she would give birth to the Messiah. Still she replied, "I am willing to accept whatever [God] wants." Her life was hardly one of comfort, especially as she watched her son being crucified. But she moved with God's desires, overcoming obstacles and playing a critical part in establishing the dream of the kingdom.

Not many Christians are like Mary in moving beyond their comfort zones. Instead of trusting God and saying, "I'm open to whatever you want," their quick response is, "I can't do that." An internal voice seems to blurt out:

- "I can't learn another language."
- "I can't overcome this temptation."
- "I can't go back to school."
- "I can't make new friends."

- "I can't change my job."
- "I can't make this marriage work."

List 10 spiritually related "I can'ts" to which you have more or less agreed:

1. _____
2. _____
3. _____
4. _____
5. _____
6. _____
7. _____
8. _____
9. _____
10. _____

Now go back and cross off the list any statements that aren't really true. This exercise helps you move out of a comfort zone that has choked in infancy some of the dreams God wants you to receive from him.

Too many of our *can'ts* aren't real. We put all kinds of restrictions on God's chal lenges to us. We unconsciously respond, *Be aware that I won't say yes, Jesus, if doing so requires much time or energy or money or a change from the way I presently live.* We don't trust God to have our best interests at heart when he comes to us with an assignment.

Going for the gulp involves opening yourself to fear, yes. But you might also experience surprise and delight because you suddenly realize that God has acted in such a wonderful way as to take your breath away.

- Keep current with your daily journal pages, and read chapter 7 in *Never Too Late to Dream.*
- Continue to embrace the new name you believe God has given you (Application 1, p. 12).
- Record your daily God Hunt sightings on pages 40–41 (Application 2, p. 19).
- Seek God's input on your godly goal (Application 3, p. 27).
- Pray daily the Daring to Dream Again Prayer (Application 4, p. 36).
- Continue to widen your circle of unlikely friends by considering any prejudi cial behavior that needs to change (Application 5, p. 45).
- Work on becoming a world-class Christian by trying to meet someone from your chosen region, country, or people-group. Also personalize ways in which God might involve you in his dreams for that area (Application 6, p. 56).

MONDAY DAY 44

Theme 7: **To dare to dream again, move with God beyond your comfort zones**

Apply the Scriptures

1. Through the process of Jesus' death, these two men were profoundly changed. Why was Joseph of Arimathea a secret disciple?

_____

2. Why do you think Nicodemus had come to Jesus by night instead of by day (see John 3:1–2)?

_____

_____

3. What did these men, both members of the Jewish high council, risk by asking a public official for the privilege of burying Christ?

_____

_____

4. When Joseph and Nicodemus broke out of their comfort zones, how did God's kingdom benefit?

_____

5. Obviously God nudged these men to participate in his kingdom dream. In what ways—large or small—do you sense God nudging you to become involved in his cause?

_____

_____

_____

❑ I am reading chapter 7 in *Never Too Late to Dream*.
❑ I have listed 10 spiritually related "I can'ts" and marked the ones that aren't really true (see the previous page).

Theme 7: **To dare to dream again, move with God beyond your comfort zone**

Apply the Scriptures

1. This man was having trouble letting go of a comfort zone. What was it?

_____

2. What did he miss out on?

_____

3. In what ways are you hearing Christ encouraging you to let go of something to follow his dreams for you?

_____

_____

4. What first step can you take to begin to respond to that challenge?

_____

_____

5. Notice the glorious contrast between the rich ruler and Peter, who said, "We have left all we had to follow you." What did Jesus say his disciples would gain as a result?

_____

_____

❏ I am attempting to meet someone from my region, country, or people-group (Application 6, p. 56).
❏ I am considering other ways to keep the Adventure going (see pp. 76–77).
❏ I am considering how my prejudicial behavior should change (Application 5, p. 45).

Go Deeper: Read Isaiah 40:27–31 on daring to dream again.

WEDNESDAY DAY 46

Theme 7: To dare to dream again, move with God beyond your comfort zones

Apply the Scriptures

1. Usually we picture Christ traveling with twelve male disciples. What were these women doing, and what roles did they play?

_____

_____

_____

2. Whom did Joanna's husband work for, and what was his job?

_____

3. Joanna probably gave up a comfortable situation to travel with and support Jesus. What might be a comfort zone of yours that could keep you from following God's dreams for you?

_____

4. Have you ever sensed God calling you to serve him in a way you knew others would question? When?

_____

_____

5. Reread Luke 24:9–10. What do these verses show us about the women's commitment to Jesus?

_____

_____

❑ I have read chapter 7 in *Never Too Late to Dream.*
❑ I am recording my God Hunt sightings on pages 40–41.
❑ I am reviewing my Scripture memory work (Philippians 3:12–14).

Theme 7: **To dare to dream again, move with God beyond your comfort zones**

Apply the Scriptures

1. How did this confusing test threaten the God-given dream that Abraham would be the father of many nations?

   _____

   _____

2. Use three words to describe the emotions Abraham must have been feeling as he left his comfort zone and journeyed to Moriah.

   _____

   _____

3. God spared Abraham the pain of sacrificing Isaac, but he chose not to spare himself the sacrifice of his own Son. What emotions must our heavenly Father have felt as he anticipated Jesus' crucifixion?

   _____

   _____

4. Is God presently testing your faith in a way that makes you gulp? If so, how?

   _____

   _____

5. If Abraham were doing this Adventure, which of the four God Hunt sighting categories might he have used to describe his discovery of the ram caught in the thicket (see p. 20)?

   _____

❑ I am learning to "go for the gulp" (Application 7, p. 65).

FRIDAY DAY 48

Theme 8: To dare to dream again, believe that with God all things are possible

Theme 8 runs Friday–Sunday, Days 48–50

Apply the Scriptures

1. Name a time when you wondered if God had forsaken you, even as you were trying to be faithful to him.

   _____

2. Many Bible scholars believe that Jesus was quoting from Psalm 22. Read the entire psalm (out loud, if possible). Which words might have helped Christ endure his suffering?

   _____

3. Scattered throughout this psalm are phrases that express Christ's experience on the cross. What are some of those?

   _____

   _____

   _____

4. What phrases in this psalm give you hope that with God all things are possible?

   _____

   _____

   _____

5. What is a concern you have that sometimes makes you question that with God all things are possible?

   _____

❑ I am personalizing ways in which God might involve me in my targeted region, country, or people-group (p. 57).

Theme 8: **To dare to dream again, believe that with God all things are possible**

Apply the Scriptures

1. If someone said to Joseph and the two Marys, "Remember, with God all things are possible," how might they have responded?

_____

2. What barriers were put into place to keep people from taking Christ's body and claiming he had risen from the dead?

_____

_____

3. Even without the barriers, why was it unlikely that the disciples would try to steal the body?

_____

_____

4. What seemingly impossible event would have to happen to get Christ's disciples to dare to dream God's kingdom dream again?

_____

5. After daring to dream again for seven weeks, are there still barriers that keep you from believing that with God all things are possible? Explain your answer

_____

_____

❏ I am reading chapter 8 in _Never Too Late to Dream_.
❏ I have shared my Adventure experience with Mainstay (see p. 79).

Go Deeper: Read Ephesians 1:15–23 on daring to dream again.

Read **John 20:24–31**

SUNDAY DAY 50

Theme 8: To dare to dream again, believe that with God all things are possible

Commentary on Theme 8

You know you're getting old when you stop dreaming. You're just staying alive to stay alive. By this standard, some people act old even when they're young.

Apart from Christ, we would have no worthy dreams. He's the One who modeled for us what life is really about: bringing God pleasure through our love for him, and making the world more like heaven by showing Christlike love for others. By his death and resurrection, our Lord made dreaming worthwhile dreams possible for everyone.

Jesus believed that with God all things are possible, even rising from the dead. So he willingly went to the cross. He wasn't immobilized by negative thinking.

You have come a long way over the past seven weeks of this Adventure. Don't allow the enemy to cause you to doubt. Believe that with God all things are possible. Stay young in spirit and continue daring to dream.

Apply the Scriptures

1. Do you identify with Thomas? If so, why?

   _____

2. What kinds of statements have you made or heard that mirror the words of Thomas in verse 25?

   _____

3. Which of Jesus' words to Thomas do you especially relate to?

   _____

4. Thomas came to understand that with God all things are possible. How is God stretching your thinking in this regard?

   _____

   _____

5. Now that the Adventure is over, what dream does God want to renew in you?

   _____

   _____

❑ I have read chapter 8 in *Never Too Late to Dream.*

SERMON NOTES

Theme 8: **To dare to dream again, believe that with God all things are possible**

_____

_____

_____

_____

_____

_____

_____

_____

_____

_____

_____

_____

_____

_____

_____

_____

_____

_____

_____

_____

_____

_____

_____

_____

_____

Adventure Application 8
Begin Dreaming Again

Jesus knew that with God all things are possible, even resurrection from the dead. This was such a part of his thinking that he rarely focused on the negative aspects of his mission. In his great concern for us, he overcame all the barriers we face and made it possible for us to dare to dream again.

It would be ridiculous to complete a Spiritual Adventure of 50 days titled "Daring to Dream Again" and not have the risen Christ open your eyes to what could unfold as you follow him more closely.

In the past seven weeks you have learned to:
- Let God heal your painful past.
- Discover God's present involvement in your life.
- Establish godly goals for your future.
- Empower everything you do for God with prayer.
- Confront your ungodly prejudices.
- Identify with God's heart for the world.
- Move with God beyond your comfort zones.

Now it's time to:
- Believe that with God all things are possible.
- *Begin dreaming again!*

What is it that God wants to whisper in your heart? Be open to his Spirit. Don't let "That's impossible" thoughts ruin the possibility that something wonderful can be birthed in your soul. This is not a time for doubt. Instead, it's a rare moment in which you can receive from the Lord a vision of what your life could be in the days and weeks and months and years ahead—if you stay close to him.

Let the Lord finish this sentence for you. "Dare to dream again, [your name]; see what I see:

_____

_____

_____

_____."

- Read chapter 8 in *Never Too Late to Dream*.
- Get God's input on your godly goal (Application 3, p. 27).
- Now that you've finished the Adventure, consider how you could continue the healthy spiritual habits you've developed. For suggestions, see page 63.

Are you pleased with the spiritual progress God has allowed you to make during this 50-Day Adventure? Or would you like a fresh start at completing an Adventure and developing healthy spiritual habits such as Bible reading, prayer, and reaching out to others? Here are six studies worth considering to help you take the next step in your relationship with Christ.

Daring to Dream Again
Overcoming Barriers That Hold You Back

An excellent option is to repeat the Adventure you've just finished. Our busy lives can make it hard to get maximum benefit from an Adventure the first time through. With all the Scripture readings and application suggestions packed into the journal, there's ample material for a second round. You'll gain new insights into the eight Adventure themes and have the chance to focus on particular application steps to really make them stick.

More than Survivors
What It Takes to Thrive Spiritually

Are you hanging on to faith by your fingernails? Do you get frustrated when you settle for the mediocre? Learn just what it takes to thrive as a Christian in this Adventure, as you delve into the lives of eight Bible heroes and examine eight principles for spiritual durability. You'll learn biblical truths and form new habits that will stick with you for years to come, while you live your life as more than a mere survivor.

More than Survivors Adult Journal and *Soul Alert* Adventure Guidebook—$10

Seeing the Unseen Christ
How His Presence Transforms Life

Are you someone who admits that your spiritual sight isn't as sharp as you'd like? That if Jesus is present every Sunday in church, you're not sure where he sits? Or that experiencing his presence the rest of the week is like trying to read the smallest line on an eye chart? If that's the case, you'll find this Spiritual Adventure a godsend. Discover eight ways to practice the presence of Christ on Sundays and beyond.

Seeing the Unseen Christ Adult Journal, *The Unseen Guest* Adventure Guidebook, and *The Little Scripture Pack for Reversing Self-Destructive Patterns*—$10

Celebrate Jesus!
Discover What Makes Him Attractive to So Many People

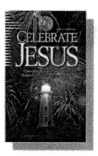

Jesus still piques the interest of committed Christians, avowed atheists, and everyone in between. Obviously, Jesus' character gives us the clues as to why he's been admired by so many so often. This Adventure focuses on eight characteristics that make Jesus attractive and helps you share him with others in practical, creative ways.

Celebrate Jesus! Adult Journal, *Jesus: The People's Choice* Adventure Guidebook, and *The Celebrate People Little Scripture Pack*—$10

Promises Worth Keeping
Resolving to Live What We Say We Believe

Men aren't the only ones who need to learn to keep their promises. Everyone—male, female, married, single, old, young—can use help in this area. In this Adventure based on the promises of the Promise Keepers Movement, you'll learn eight biblical concepts designed to help all Christians live what they say they believe.

Promises Worth Keeping Adult Journal, *People of Promise* Adventure Guidebook, and *The Little Scripture Pack for Practicing Purity*—$10

The Church You've Always Longed For
What You Can Do to Make It Happen

Church can be the high point of your week! In this 50-Day Spiritual Adventure, you'll discover biblical ways to contribute to building the church you've always longed for.

The Church You've Always Longed For Adult Journal and the *I Like Church, But . . .* Adventure Guidebook—$10

To order any of these Adventures, use the form on page 78 or call weekdays: 1-800-224-2735 (U.S.), 1-800-461-4114 (Canada). You may also purchase these materials online:
www.teamsundays.org/adventure.

Item	Title	Retail	Qty	Total
Daring to Dream Again Resources				
0310	Adult Journal	7.00	___	___
0350	Adult Journal in Large Print	7.00	___	___
1975	Never Too Late to Dream Adventure Guidebook	7.00	___	___
0320	Student Journal	7.00	___	___
0330	Children's Journal (Grades 3–6)	7.00	___	___
0340	Children's Activity Book (Grades K–2)	7.00	___	___
3306	Small Group Leader's Guide	8.00	___	___
8463	Adventure Video (sermon booster/drama/discussion)	30.00	___	___
Other Adventure Resources				
5888	More than Survivors Adult Journal & Guidebook	10.00	___	___
5771	Seeing the Unseen Christ Adult Journal, Guidebook, & Scripture Pack	10.00	___	___
5861	Celebrate Jesus! Adult Journal, Guidebook, & Scripture Pack	10.00	___	___
5859	Promises Worth Keeping Adult Journal, Guidebook, & Scripture Pack	10.00	___	___
5770	The Church You've Always . . . Adult Journal & Guidebook	10.00	___	___

SUBTOTAL ☐

Add 10% for UPS shipping/handling ($4.00 minimum) ☐

Illinois residents add 7% sales tax ☐

TOTAL AMOUNT ENCLOSED ☐

Check payment method: ☐ Check ☐ Visa ☐ MasterCard ☐ AmEx
☐ Discover ☐ Check-by-Phone

Name _____

Street Address* _____City_____

State/Prov _____ Zip/Code _____Phone (___) _____

Church Name _____

Credit Card # _____ Exp. Date_____

Signature _____

*Note: UPS will not deliver to a P.O. Box.

Mail this order form and make checks payable to:

In Canada:

Mainstay Church Resources   **The Chapel Ministries**
P.O. Box 30   920 Brant St., Unit 15
Wheaton, IL 60189-0030   Burlington, ON L7R 4J1

You can also order these resources by calling **1-800-224-2735** (U.S.), **1-800-461-4114** (Canada), or by visiting us online at **www.teamsundays.org/adventure.**

MO83

Printed in the United States
202078BV00002B/1-96/A